Colors

by Tristan Horrom
illustrated by Diane Blasius

Pre-Decodable 8

McGraw Hill Education

Bothell, WA • Chicago, IL • Columbus, OH • New York, NY

MHEonline.com

Send all inquiries to:
McGraw-Hill Education
8787 Orion Place
Columbus, OH 43240

ISBN: 978-0-02-135385-9
MHID: 0-02-135385-9

Printed in China

9 10 11 12 13 DSS 28 27 26 25 24

He had

brown

bumps

.

He had  .

white fur

He had  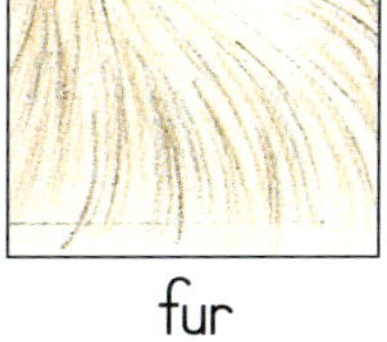.

black fur

He had  .

blue feathers

He had  .

red feathers

He had   !

rainbow feathers